D1606911

SEA STAR

 S U S A N H . G R A Y

CHERRY
LAKE
Publishing

Published in the United States of America by Cherry Lake Publishing
Ann Arbor, Michigan
www.cherrylakepublishing.com

Consultants: Dominique A. Didier, PhD, Associate Professor, Department of Biology, Millersville University;
Marla Conn, ReadAbility, Inc.
Book design: Sleeping Bear Press

Photo Credits: ©NatureDiver/Shutterstock Images, cover, 1, 19; ©Song Heming/Shutterstock Images, 5; ©lauraslens/
Shutterstock Images, 7; ©Vilainecrevette/Shutterstock Images, 9; ©Dorling Kindersley/Thinkstock, 10; ©Greg
Amptman/Shutterstock Images, 12; ©scubaluna/Shutterstock Images, 13; ©Krzysztof Wiktor/Shutterstock Images, 14;
©almondd/Shutterstock Images, 15; ©peter herbig/Thinkstock, 17; ©walkdragon/Shutterstock Images, 21; ©Jerry
Kirkhart/http://www.flickr.com/CC-BY-2.0, 22; ©Jupiterimages/Thinkstock, 23, 25; ©ejeck/Thinkstock, 27; ©tae208/
Shutterstock Images, 29

Library of Congress Cataloging-in-Publication Data

Gray, Susan Heinrichs, author.
Sea star / by Susan H. Gray.
    pages cm. — (Exploring our oceans)
  Summary: "Discover facts about sea stars, including physical features, habitat, life cycle, food,
  and threats to these ocean creatures. Photos, captions, and keywords supplement the narrative of
  this informational text"—Provided by publisher.
  Audience: Age 8-12.
  Audience: Grades 4 to 6.
  ISBN 978-1-63188-023-0 (hardcover)—ISBN 978-1-63188-066-7 (pbk.)—ISBN 978-1-63188-109-1 (pdf)—
  ISBN 978-1-63188-152-7 (ebook) 1. Starfishes—Juvenile literature. I. Title. II. Title: Sea star. III.
  Series: 21st century skills library. Exploring our oceans.

  QL384.A8G73 2015
  593.9'3—dc23   2014005460

Cherry Lake Publishing would like to acknowledge the work of
The Partnership for 21st Century Skills. Please visit www.p21.org
for more information.

Printed in the United States of America
Corporate Graphics Inc.

ABOUT THE AUTHOR

Susan H. Gray has a master's degree in zoology. She has worked in research and has taught college-
level science classes. Susan has also written more than 140 science and reference books, but
especially likes to write about animals. She and her husband, Michael, live in Cabot, Arkansas.

TABLE OF CONTENTS

No Luck!

The sea star began to sense something in the water. It was the smell of food. The animal began creeping toward it.

Soon it came upon a group of **scallops**. The sea star's arm gently touched one scallop. But the prey slammed its shell closed and jerked out of harm's way. The sea star continued on to the next scallop. It, too, snapped shut and jumped away. Suddenly, all of the other scallops got the same idea. Shells began clapping shut. In no time, they had all fled, leaving the sea star alone.

[21ST CENTURY SKILLS LIBRARY]

The sea star stopped moving. The smell of food was not so strong now. Perhaps it would have better luck next time.

Sea stars live underwater, in warm and cold climates.

Sea stars, or starfish, live in every one of the world's oceans. They are found in warm tropical waters. They also **thrive** in ice-cold polar seas. Some prefer to creep along the seafloor or over coral reefs. Others live on sandy or muddy bottoms. Still others prefer rocky areas.

Some, such as the purple sea star, live in an area called the intertidal zone. This is an area along the seashore. When the seawater rises at high tide, the area is covered by water. When the water goes back down at low tide, the area is exposed to the air.

GO DEEPER

SEA STARS CANNOT LIVE IN LAKES OR RIVERS. WHY DO YOU THINK THAT IS?

Sea stars can cling to rocks and coral.

THE SEA STAR'S BODY

There are around 1,900 different **species** of sea stars known today. Each one has a round disc at the center of its body. Arms stick out from the disc. Although most sea stars have five arms, some have up to 50!

Starfish do not have bones. But they do have hundreds of small, hard plates throughout their bodies. These plates are called ossicles. They provide strength and support.

Most species have a flattened body. The common starfish is about as thick as a person's hand. The spiny cushion sea star looks a bit puffy, like a pillow. And the pin cushion sea star looks like a five-sided lump of dough.

Cushion starfish live on the ocean floor.

BODY DIAGRAM

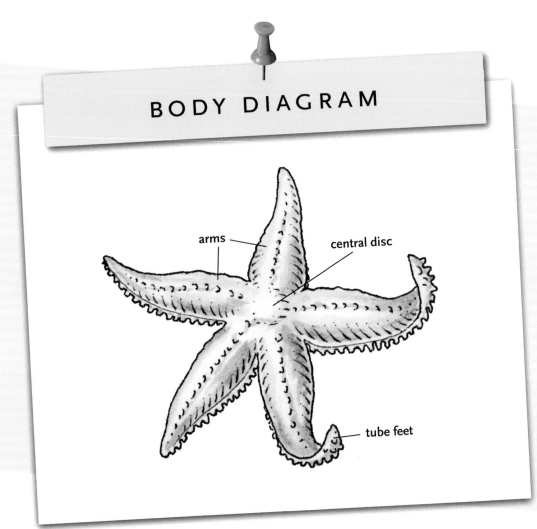

A sea star uses its arms to sense things from all directions.

Sea stars belong to a large group of animals called **echinoderms**. Other echinoderms are sea urchins and sea cucumbers. Echinoderms have rough skin that is covered with spines. Between the spines of sea stars are small, soft gills. These organs are used for breathing.

Sea stars have no front end and no back end. Their body parts are arranged in a circle. Scientists call this radial symmetry. Creatures with radial symmetry can sense things from all directions. They can also travel in any direction at any time.

Sea stars have no head and no brain. Inside the disc, they have a ring of nerves. Other nerves branch out from the ring and run down the arms. The nerves send signals that operate the starfish's muscles.

Nerves also pick up information from the environment. At the tip of each arm is an eyespot. It detects different intensities of light. On the underside of the sea star are thousands of tiny feet. They have sensors that detect food.

Most sea stars have five arms, but some have more.

The sea star moves by using its feet. The animal has an incredible system for operating its feet. Each foot is a tiny, delicate tube. Seawater is pushed into each tube, which stretches it. The feet touch down on a surface, and their tips attach to it. When this happens, the water is forced away from the tubes. This shortens the feet. As the feet shorten, the sea star is pulled forward. The tubes fill back up with water, and the sea star stops moving. The tips release and stick to a new surface nearby.

The tips at the end of the sea star's
tube feet help it cling to rocks.

The sea star's mouth is on the underside, in the center of the disc. It leads into a short passageway and then into the stomach. The sea star also has reproductive organs. These are located in the arms. They produce **sperm** cells in males and egg cells in females. 🦈

This photograph shows the underside of a sea star as it clings to a glass pane.

[21ST CENTURY SKILLS LIBRARY]

Sea urchins and sea stars are both echinoderms.

LOOK AGAIN

THE SEA URCHIN IS AN ECHINODERM. WHAT FEATURES DOES IT SHARE WITH SEA STARS?

SEA STAR FOOD

Sea stars are both predators and **scavengers**. Because they are slow movers, sea stars hunt other slow-moving animals. They feed on living snails and worms. They also eat **bivalves**, such as clams, oysters, and scallops. The bivalves have soft, meaty bodies. They are enclosed between two halves of a shell. Their strong muscles can keep the shells tightly closed.

But sea stars are often stronger than the bivalves. They creep slowly over the shelled animals. They arch

This sea star will have to pull open the shell of its prey before it can eat the soft body inside.

their bodies over their prey. The ends of their tube feet attach and hold the shells in a mighty grip. Once the sea star clamps onto the bivalve, it begins to force the bivalve's shell open. Just a crack is all it needs.

As soon as the shell is barely opened, the predator does something amazing. The lower chamber of its stomach moves out of its body. While still attached to the sea star, the stomach oozes out through its mouth. It squeezes through the crack in the bivalve's shell. It then releases digestive juices. The juices break down the bivalve's tissues, which then slide into the sea star's stomach. When the animal is finished eating, its stomach draws away and returns to the sea star's body.

LOOK AGAIN

LOOK CLOSELY AT THIS PHOTOGRAPH OF A SEA STAR WITH MANY ARMS.
DO YOU THINK IT IS STRONGER THAN A SEA STAR WITH FEWER ARMS?

A Star Is Born

Many sea stars are ready to **reproduce** by the time they are one or two years old. At this time, females release millions of egg cells into the water. Likewise, males release millions of sperm cells. Each time an egg unites with a sperm, a new, tiny individual is formed.

At first, the little sea star looks nothing like its parents. It's not even shaped like a star. Instead, it first develops into a ball of cells and floats freely in the water. As it grows, it develops a mouth and short hairlike structures called cilia.

[21ST CENTURY SKILLS LIBRARY]

The cilia sweep floating, microscopic food particles into the mouth. At this stage, the starfish is called a larva.

This young sea star looks just like a small adult.

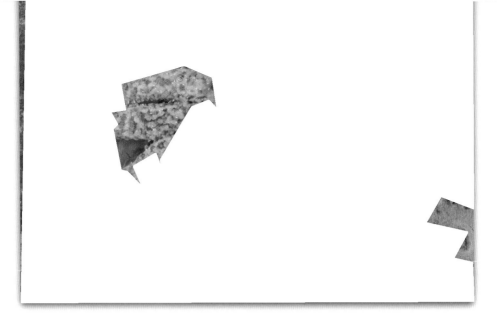

Sometimes a sea star may lose an arm, but it will grow back.

The larva continues to float, often for weeks. During this time, its little body goes through many changes. Eventually, it settles on the seafloor. There, it develops into a small starfish, complete with radial symmetry.

Sea stars also have another way of reproducing. They do this without any egg or sperm cells at all. They create entirely new animals from parts of existing ones.

This is how it works. Sometimes, sea stars are damaged by predators or by encounters with humans. Their arms may be torn away, sometimes with small portions of their disks. You may think this would kill the animal. But instead, those pieces remain alive.

A predator may have torn off one of this sea star's arms.

They begin to grow the rest of the disk. New arms begin to sprout from the disk. Eventually, where there was one damaged starfish to begin with, there now may be five new ones!

Some sea stars can actually split themselves in two! The split may be uneven, with one new starfish having more arms than the other. But those new starfish continue to grow and might even split again later.

Each of a sea star's arms is not always the same length.

LOOK AGAIN

LOOK CLOSELY AT THIS PHOTOGRAPH OF A SEA STAR. WHY DO YOU THINK THIS SEA STAR HAS SOME ARMS THAT ARE SHORTER THAN OTHERS?

SURVIVING AND THRIVING

Some sea creatures do eat sea stars, despite their rough skin and spines. Predators include other starfish species, sea otters, gulls, and sharks.

However, sea stars have ways of protecting themselves. Most have rough skin that is difficult to chew and digest. Some sea stars just taste bad. Others have **toxic** chemicals in their bodies that can make predators sick. Still others, like the slime star, put out gobs of slime. Predators simply don't want to deal with it. And the crown-of-thorns starfish is so spiny, most animals don't even *think* of eating it. For similar reasons, most people do not eat starfish.

In some parts of the world, though, people collect them for souvenirs. And in some regions, people kill them as pests. Oyster farmers, for example, try to get rid these echinoderms. If a sea star invades an oyster bed, it can eat up to 15 young oysters a day.

Sea stars don't have many predators, but one is the seagull.

Near Australia, some sea stars have created problems. The northern Pacific sea star has nearly wiped out one type of fish by eating its eggs. And the crown-of-thorns starfish damages coral reefs by eating the soft coral animals.

Scientists are working on ways to control sea star populations. They know they must plan carefully and not make things worse. Everyone wants to see the fish and coral reefs do well. But they also want to make sure the sea stars thrive, too.

THINK ABOUT IT

WHY CAN'T SCIENTISTS POISON JUST THE SEA STARS THAT ARE CAUSING DAMAGE?

The crown-of-thorns starfish is spiny enough to scare away other animals.

THINK ABOUT IT

- In chapter 1, you learned that some sea stars live in the intertidal zone. What might be some of the problems animals face by living in this zone?

- Why do you think some scientists prefer the term sea star over starfish?

- Chapter 4 describes how sea stars regrow body parts. Can you name any land animals that do this?

- People buy sea stars as souvenirs and to decorate their homes. Do you think this reduces the sea star populations very much? Why or why not?

LEARN MORE

FURTHER READING

Blaxland, Beth. *Sea Stars, Sea Urchins, and Their Relatives*. New York: Chelsea Clubhouse, 2002.

Gilpin, Daniel. *Starfish, Urchins & Other Echinoderms*. North Mankato, MN: Compass Point Books, 2006.

Hoyt, Erich. *Weird Sea Creatures*. Richmond Hill, ON: Firefly Books, 2013.

WEB SITES

How Stuff Works—Starfish
http://animal.discovery.com/marine-life/starfish-info.htm
Learn about sea stars, their lives, and their habits at this very informative Web site.

National Geographic Kids—Sea Stars
http://kids.nationalgeographic.com/kids/animals/creaturefeature/sea-stars
Watch a video on sea stars, find information about them, and see a map showing where they live.

GLOSSARY

bivalves (BYE-valvz) animals, such as oysters and clams, that have a two-part hinged shell

echinoderms (ih-KYE-nuh-durmz) animals that have spiny skin

reproduce (ree-pruh-DOOS) to produce one or more new individuals of the same species

scallops (SKAH-luhps) shellfish with meaty bodies and hinged shells

scavengers (SKAV-in-jerz) animals that eat dead animals

species (SPEE-sheez) one type, or kind, of plant or animal

sperm (SPURM) male reproductive cell

thrive (THRYV) to do very well, or to be successful

toxic (TAHK-sik) poisonous

INDEX